When a fortune teller told young Elizabeth Bowes-Lyon that she would be Queen, the lively seven-year-old was dismissive, saying 'Who wants to be Queen anyway?'

This is the story of her chance meeting with Prince Albert and how they fell in love and married. It tells how, through a twist of fate, Elizabeth did indeed become Queen and overcome the tragedies of war and personal bereavement to become Britain's beloved Queen Mother.

Topham Picture Library

Topham Picture Library

AN UNLIKELY MATCH

HE WAS SHY AND RETIRING, SHE WAS THE LIFE AND SOUL OF ANY PARTY. BUT THE START OF THE LOVE AFFAIR BETWEEN PRINCE ALBERT AND ELIZABETH BOWES-LYON PROVED BEYOND DOUBT THAT OPPOSITES ATTRACT

Elizabeth inset *was a vivacious, pretty little girl, adored by her parents and family. In the cold, uninviting atmosphere at York House near Sandringham, Bertie* below *was badly neglected by his nurses and ignored by his father*

ILN Picture Library

Hulton-Deutsch Collection

BORN ON 4 AUGUST 1900, IN LONDON, THE Honourable Elizabeth Angela Marguerite Bowes-Lyon spent an idyllic childhood, within a large and loving family and among beautiful surroundings. Eight elder sisters and brothers preceded her: Violet, Mary, Patrick, John, Alexander, Fergus, Rose and Michael. Sadly, Violet died, aged 11, of diphtheria, before Elizabeth was born. David was born two years later in 1902 – he called her 'Buffy' and they were inseparable companions at their Hertfordshire home in St Paul's Walden Bury.

Elizabeth was adored by her father, Claude Bowes-Lyon, who was descended from King Robert II of Scotland. On the death of his father in 1904, he became the 14th Earl of Strathmore and Kinghorne. Elizabeth's mother, Lady Strathmore, formerly Nina Cecilia Cavendish-Bentinck, was the granddaughter of the Duke of Portland and related to many great English families.

The influence of this enlightened and intelligent lady was to serve Elizabeth well in later life. And, unusual for the times, Lady Strathmore took an active interest in bringing up and educating her children, especially the two younger ones, Elizabeth and David – 'the two Benjamins' as they were called.

Happy days

Life was privileged for the family, which divided its time between its principal home, St Paul's Walden Bury in Hertfordshire, Streatlam Castle in Durham, Glamis – a castle in Scotland – and the London house in St James's Square.

From an early age, Elizabeth was used to adult company and not awed by it. 'Shall us sit and talk?' she suggested as she poured tea for a guest when she was only six. But it was not all precocious charm. Elizabeth and David could get up to mischief like any other children: they would set a balloon in front of a motor car for an already nervous chauffeur to drive over and burst. Nor were they averse to 'repelling raiders', as they called it, by dousing newcomers at the main door with a torrent of water from above.

The unhappy Prince

The boy who would one day become King George VI could not have had a more different childhood. Albert Frederick Arthur George picked a most inauspicious day to be born on in 1895. 14 December each year was a double Royal death anniversary and a day of mourning for the entire Royal Family. Queen Victoria had set aside this sacred day, 34 years ago, to fervently mourn not only the death of her adored husband, Albert, but also, since 1878, the death of her daughter, Princess Alice.

Having inadvertently started off on the wrong foot, the baby was to develop into an intensely sensitive and highly strung young child, but the young Prince's parents, the Duke and Duchess of York (later King George V and Queen Mary) were singularly unqualified to provide the warmth and understanding that he so badly needed.

It was not that they lacked parental affection, but their own inhibitions and the then conventions of strict child rearing among the upper classes meant that they could not build a happy and intimate relationship with their children.

The young Prince Albert, or Bertie as he was always known, was also overshadowed on either side by his elder and already charming brother, David (later Edward VIII and the Duke of Windsor) just 18 months his senior, and by his ebullient younger sister, Mary, who was 16 months younger. Three more brothers followed: Prince Henry (later Duke of Gloucester) who was born in 1900, Prince George (later Duke of Kent) born in 1902, and Prince John, who was born in 1905. Unfortunately, Prince John suffered from epilepsy and lived segregated for the last two years of his life until he died aged 14.

Childhood miseries

Insensitive nursemaids did little to mitigate poor Bertie's difficult babyhood. Given the bottle while jolted around in a badly sprung carriage, he suffered severe gastric distress, which plagued him always. The affection he so desperately needed was available only at the house of his grandfather, the Prince of Wales – who had become King in 1901.

To add to poor Bertie's burdens, when he began to write, he was forced to use his right hand even though he was naturally inclined to use the left. This probably led him to develop the debilitating stammer that he had until late in life. And to top it all, he was forced to wear splints — even at night — to corrcct his inherited knock knees until he was reduced to tears by the pain. Yet, he bravely wrote to his mother, 'I expect I shall get used to them.' After being tutored privately, at 13 Bertie went to join David at the Royal Naval College at Osborne on the Isle of Wight. As his father

Syndication International

🜲 Above *Young Bertie (standing on left with his father, George V) often went to Osborne House on the Isle of Wight to visit his great-grandmother, Queen Victoria*

🜲 Below *Elizabeth, aged nine, with her favourite brother David. Both children delighted in wearing fancy dress, as for this dancing lesson at Glamis Castle*

Woodmansterne

Syndication International

3

Hulton-Deutsch Collection

Popperfoto

♛ *Bertie aged ten wearing his favourite sailor suit*

♛ *Happy holidays — Bertie (left) and brother David on the Isle of Wight*

Popperfoto

♛ *Bertie, sister Mary and brothers, Henry and David*

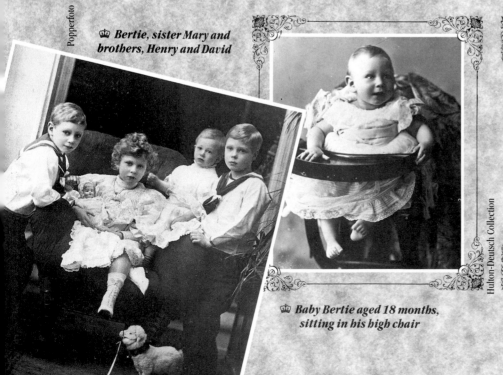

Hulton-Deutsch Collection

♛ *Baby Bertie aged 18 months, sitting in his high chair*

Popperfoto

♛ *Bertie, the Marquise de Hautpont and sister Mary at Cowes*

Album
Elizabeth

♚ *A favourite childhood companion of Elizabeth's – her pony 'Bobs'*

♚ *Elizabeth Bowes-Lyon – aged seven years*

♚ *Already a young beauty, Elizabeth aged 14 years*

♚ *Elizabeth and brother David enjoying a garden party at Glamis*

♚ *An attractive miniature of Elizabeth as a young girl*

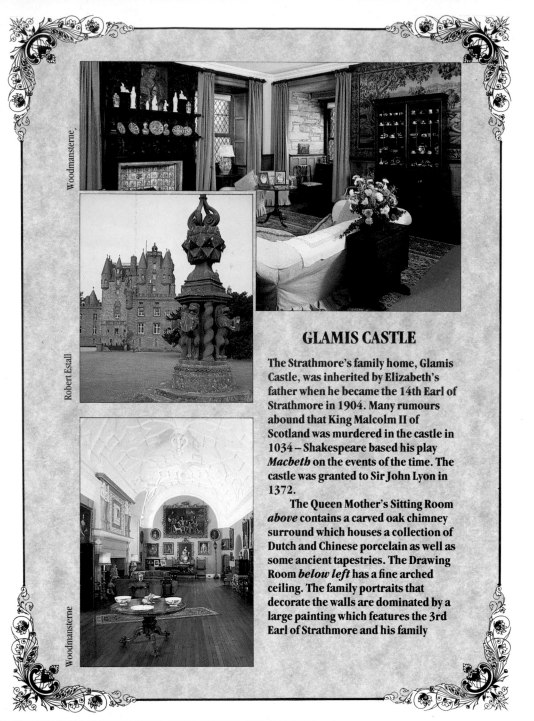

Woodmansterne.

Robert Estall

Woodmansterne

GLAMIS CASTLE

The Strathmore's family home, Glamis Castle, was inherited by Elizabeth's father when he became the 14th Earl of Strathmore in 1904. Many rumours abound that King Malcolm II of Scotland was murdered in the castle in 1034 – Shakespeare based his play *Macbeth* on the events of the time. The castle was granted to Sir John Lyon in 1372.

The Queen Mother's Sitting Room *above* contains a carved oak chimney surround which houses a collection of Dutch and Chinese porcelain as well as some ancient tapestries. The Drawing Room *below left* has a fine arched ceiling. The family portraits that decorate the walls are dominated by a large painting which features the 3rd Earl of Strathmore and his family

♛ *Bertie, pictured with his sister Mary on a scenic railway at Earl's Court, managed to have some occasional moments of fun in his teenage years. Later, Mary was to play Cupid to the lovers when she arranged for the two of them to meet at Buckingham Palace. She was also instrumental in persuading Elizabeth to accept her brother's proposal of marriage*

Popperfoto

had insisted that he should be treated exactly the same as any other cadet, he was given the full rough treatment of bullying and was teased for his stammer.

Academically, he did not shine, achieving sixty-eighth position in a class of sixty eight at the end of the final term. But he made up for it by being commended for his 'integrity and courage' and was soon liked by all for his sense of fun and mischief.

After two years at the Dartmouth Royal Naval College, Bertie was put to sea on the cruiser *Cumberland* when he was 17.

When World War I broke out, Bertie was serving aboard HMS *Collingwood* as a midshipman. But it was not his destiny to prove himself in active service for a while, for soon after, he fell ill with appendicitis, and for much of the war he was visited by the ghost of his childhood misery, the 'infernal indigestion', as he called it. He did see action at the Battle of Jutland in May 1916, however, after which he fell severely ill again with a duodenal ulcer. He was relieved to have experienced combat for the first time, however. 'I never experienced any fear of shells or anything else,' he announced proudly. The illness dogged him though and it became clear that he would need surgery.

After he was operated on, it was decided it would be best for him to leave the Navy; instead, he joined the naval wing of the Air Force at Cranwell in Lincolnshire.

Elizabeth's war

'Those awful four years,' was how the war appeared to Elizabeth. Tragedy struck the Bowes-Lyon household when Fergus was killed in 1915. Two years later, it seemed a double blow was to be struck when Michael was reported missing. Joyfully, however, he was soon reunited with his family.

Elizabeth was 14 when war had been declared and Glamis Castle had been turned into a convalescent hospital. Although not yet old enough to be a proper nurse, Elizabeth involved herself fully in the war effort. Not only did she crumple tissue paper to fill sleeping bags, knit and write letters dictated by the wounded soldiers, she took the compassionate and personal interest in all of them that has always been her hallmark.

It was not surprising, then, that one of the departing soldiers wrote in her autograph book: 'May the owner of this book be hung, drawn and quartered. Yes, hung in diamonds, drawn in a coach and four and quartered in the best house in the land.' A prophetic wish indeed.

COURTSHIP AND BETROTHAL

After the war, Bertie, along with his brother, Henry, spent a year at Trinity College, Cambridge, studying Bible History and the Constitution. They were not allowed to room within the college, but lived attended in a small house nearby, although like all undergraduates, they would cycle in to lectures. At the end of the year, Bertie's efforts at always trying to please his father – unlike his brother, David – were rewarded when the King conferred upon him the oldest dukedom in the land – that of Duke of York.

Love at first sight

One evening in 1920, Bertie and some friends dropped in at a dance given by Lord Farquhar in London. Dancing with James Stuart, the son of the Earl of Moray, was Elizabeth. Bertie summoned the young man to inquire who his partner was, and soon it was he who had Elizabeth in his arms.

It is said that they had actually first met at a children's party when a five-year-old Elizabeth had offered the awkward young Prince the cherries from her cake. But whether he remembered that characteristically kind gesture or not, as they danced, Bertie had already fallen in love.

Soon, he was a frequent visitor at Glamis and St Paul's, happy to be near her and in the warm and intimate atmosphere conjured up by her large family. The fact that his sister, Princess Mary, was already good friends with Elizabeth allowed him to enjoy even more of her company.

During his second visit, he wrote to his mother, 'It is delightful here and Elizabeth is very kind to me. The more I see her, the more I like her.' Queen Mary resolved to say nothing. 'Mothers should never meddle in their children's love affairs,' she wisely confided to a friend, but she did admit, 'He is always talking about her.'

Finally, she became so intrigued that she, too, made the journey to Glamis with her daughter, Mary. The Queen was impressed and sent a favourable report to her husband. Early in 1922, Princess Mary married Lord

> *'Elizabeth is very kind to me. The more I see of her, the more I like her'*
>
> THE DUKE OF YORK

Lascelles in Westminster Abbey and chose Elizabeth as one of her eight bridesmaids. Even the King was impressed by now. 'You'll be a lucky fellow if she accepts you,' he told Bertie.

Third time lucky

It was not long before Bertie plucked up his courage and proposed marriage to Elizabeth. But she took some time deciding. 'I was afraid, as royalty, never, never again to be free to think or speak or act,' she confessed.

Elizabeth refused twice. But Bertie had learnt early that things did not come easily to him unless he persevered. He proposed yet again as the couple strolled in the grounds of St Paul's Walden Bury one cold January day in 1923. This time, Elizabeth, already much warmed by his sincerity and integrity, accepted. 'I am not sure that I wasn't the most surprised of the two,' she announced when they returned to the house. For his part, Bertie was over the moon. The message was telegrammed to Sandringham in the agreed code: 'All right. Bertie.'

Bertie went down to Sandringham to ask his father's formal consent, and the Court Circular, issued on 15 January 1923, made the announcement: 'It is with the greatest pleasure that the King and Queen announce the betrothal of their beloved son the Duke of York to the Lady Elizabeth Bowes-Lyon, daughter of the Earl and Countess of Strathmore, to which union the King has gladly given his consent.' Yet, despite all the noble blood in her veins, and her ancient family tree, Elizabeth was not a member of a

♛ *After they had met, Elizabeth and Bertie spent as much time together as possible. They are pictured above at a polo match, early in 1923. Bertie was soon drawn into the warmth of the Bowes-Lyon family and he became a frequent visitor at their home. The group at Glamis Castle below includes, from the left, Elizabeth's brother David, her father, Bertie and Elizabeth. Elizabeth's mother is seated on the right. The courtship did not run completely smoothly, however. Although Elizabeth was aware of Bertie's intentions, she was worried – the responsibilities of being wife to a prince were awesome. She twice refused his proposals of marriage*

royal family. For over 200 years, the British Royal family had always married royal – and often foreign – wives. Elizabeth, as so often later, was to set a precedent and break with convention.

As the wedding date approached, guests began to arrive from all over the world – no less than five Indian Princes were installed at the Savoy Hotel. In honour of the royal occasion, the King decided to confer two very special titles – he made Bertie a Knight of the Thistle and appointed Elizabeth's father Knight Commander of the Victorian Order (KCVO).

The stage was now set for a very special occasion that would combine all the happiness of a family celebration with all the pomp and pageantry of a great Royal wedding.

♛ *Elizabeth finally accepted Bertie during a romantic walk in the woods near her family home in St Paul's Walden Bury.*

Their engagement was announced on 16 January 1923. The official picture of the couple opposite was taken the same day

The Bowes-Lyon Connection

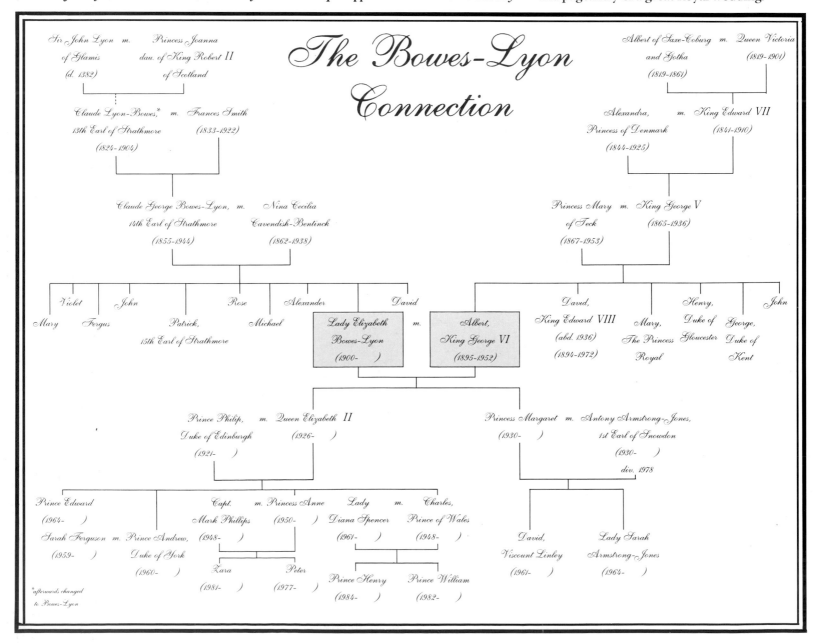

Sir John Lyon m. Princess Joanna
of Glamis   dau. of King Robert II
(d. 1382)   of Scotland

Albert of Saxe-Coburg m. Queen Victoria
and Gotha   (1819-1901)
(1819-1861)

Claude Lyon-Bowes,* m. Frances Smith
13th Earl of Strathmore   (1833-1922)
(1824-1904)

Alexandra,   m. King Edward VII
Princess of Denmark   (1841-1910)
(1844-1925)

Claude George Bowes-Lyon, m. Nina Cecilia
14th Earl of Strathmore   Cavendish-Bentinck
(1855-1944)   (1862-1938)

Princess Mary m. King George V
of Teck   (1865-1936)
(1867-1953)

Violet   John   Rose   Alexander   David

Mary   Fergus   Patrick,   Michael
15th Earl of Strathmore

Lady Elizabeth Bowes-Lyon (1900-) m. Albert, King George VI (1895-1952)

David, King Edward VIII (abd. 1936) (1894-1972)

Henry, Duke of Gloucester

Mary, The Princess Royal

George, Duke of Kent

John

Prince Philip, Duke of Edinburgh (1921-) m. Queen Elizabeth II (1926-)

Princess Margaret (1930-) m. Antony Armstrong-Jones, 1st Earl of Snowdon (1930-) div. 1978

Prince Edward (1964-)

Sarah Ferguson (1959-) m. Prince Andrew, Duke of York (1960-)

Capt. Mark Phillips (1948-) m. Princess Anne (1950-)

Lady Diana Spencer (1961-) m. Charles, Prince of Wales (1948-)

Zara (1981-)   Peter (1977-)

Prince Henry (1984-)   Prince William (1982-)

David, Viscount Linley (1961-)

Lady Sarah Armstrong-Jones (1964-)

*afterwards changed to Bowes-Lyon

STATE REGALIA

JEWELS IN THE CROWN

Each coronation sees an addition to the nation's regalia. The splendour of 12 May 1937 was no exception. Amidst the orbs and sceptres were the magnificent newly modelled crowns made especially for George VI and his Queen

THE KOH-I-NOOR

♛ A legendary diamond, which was presented to Queen Victoria in 1850 by the East India Company, the *Koh-i-Noor* or 'Mountain of Light' can be traced to the Mogul emperors of India. No English king has worn the Koh-i-Noor – it is said to bring bad luck to male rulers. Re-set for the Coronation in 1937, it is now the gorgeous centrepiece of the Queen Mother's crown

THE IMPERIAL STATE CROWN

♛ The Sceptre with the Cross *right* was made for Mary of Modena in the 17th century. The white enamelled dove, *below*, sitting on a golden orb and cross, forms the top of the Queen Consort's Ivory Rod, also made for Mary of Modena

Crown Copyright

♛ The most valuable piece of jewellery in the world, this splendid crown was re-set for the Coronation of George VI. The back of the crown *below* is equally magnificent

Crown Copyright

Crown Copyright

THE CONSORT'S RING

♛ This large ruby and diamond ring was originally worn by Queen Adelaide, wife of William IV

QUEEN ELIZABETH'S CROWN

The *Koh-i-Noor* forms a magnificent centrepiece to the crown made for Elizabeth as Queen Consort. The crown is made of platinum with detachable arches that permit it to be used as a coronet *see opposite*. Elizabeth wore it in this style at her daughter's Coronation. Below the Koh-i-Noor diamond is a 17-carat stone which was given as a loyal tribute to Queen Victoria by the Sultan of Turkey (this diamond was only worn at the Coronation). Another historic gem is the teardrop-shaped Lahore diamond in the centre of the cross at the top. Sixteen square-cut diamonds, four drops and 2,802 smaller stones entirely covering the arches and circlet complete this treasure

ILN Picture Library

TO LOVE, HONOUR AND OBEY

ON 26 APRIL 1923, A MILLION PEOPLE LINED THE STREETS TO CHEER THE ROYAL COUPLE. THE BELLS OF WESTMINSTER ABBEY RANG OUT JOYFULLY TO CELEBRATE ITS FIRST ROYAL WEDDING FOR FIVE HUNDRED YEARS

♛ The crowds cheered and the rain stopped, as if by magic, as the bride stepped out of the family home in Bruton Street, accompanied by her father. There was plenty more for the people of London to see as they crowded the streets of the capital. One of the biggest roars went up as George V and Queen Mary waved to them from their carriage on the way to the Abbey opposite

Hulton-Deutsch Collection

E VEN BEFORE THE WEDDING, THE PRESENTS came pouring in. For Elizabeth, who was usually seen to decorate her beauty with nothing more than her familiar strand of pearls with one teardrop pendant, it must have seemed like Aladdin's cave. The King offered her a suite of diamonds and turquoises, Queen Mary gave her a sapphire and diamonds from her own collection, and Queen Alexandra's present was a long rope necklace of her favourite amethysts. Her father presented her with a diamond tiara and a rope of diamonds and pearls, while her mother gave Bertie an exquisite miniature of his fiancée, looking winsome and sweet, surrounded with precious stones. He was to treasure it always.

The stage was certainly well and truly set. Everybody, from barrow boy to baronet, was set to enjoy themselves and celebrate the young couple's happiness.

A grand occasion

As Elizabeth and Lord Strathmore emerged from the tall house at 17 Bruton Street on that cold, damp Thursday, eager eyes from the crowd caught the first glimpse of what was described as 'the simplest gown ever made for a Royal Wedding.'

When Elizabeth had been a bridesmaid at Princess Mary's wedding, she could hardly have anticipated that the next Royal Wedding celebrated would be her own. Now she and her father climbed into a State landau closed against the evil drizzle and gently moved off, escorted by four mounted policemen. Lord Strathmore was resplendent in his scarlet Lord Lieutenant's uniform but he did look just a little gloomy as he prepared to give up his daughter to the rigours of royal life.

The Abbey bells pealed, and gusts of wind scattered drops of rain over the troops who lined the wedding route.

Three thousand guests were taking their places in the Abbey for the first marriage of a King's son to take place there since King Richard II had married 'Good Anne of Bohemia' in 1382.

Grandest of all in the Abbey was Queen Mary. To the music of Edward Elgar's *Imperial*

Hulton-Deutsch Collection

March, she and the King led the family procession through the Abbey. With the biggest diamond in the whole royal collection, the Star of Africa, pinned to her blue Garter sash, the aquamarine and silver tissue of her dress embroidered with the rose of York and showered with crystal drops, and with five rows of diamonds glittering at her throat, while another diamond adorned her brocade toque, she quite eclipsed the King, who wore the uniform of an Admiral of the Fleet.

Following the Royal party, the Duke arrived – a dashing figure in the full-dress uniform of Group Captain of the RAF, with the blue riband of the Garter. He was accompanied by his brothers David, the Prince of Wales, dapper in the uniform of the Grenadier Guards, and Henry, later Duke of Gloucester, in the uniform of the 10th Hussars.

Here comes the bride

Elizabeth was composed as she entered the dark Abbey on her father's arm at 11.30 am precisely. Her narrow ivory dress, shimmering

ILN Picture Library

with silver thread, was the perfect foil for her fragile beauty. Elizabeth's famous pearls were around her neck completing the gorgeous picture.

A soldier dashed into the Abbey just after Elizabeth entered, carrying the bride's tiny white silk reticule – a handkerchief bag she had abandoned in the carriage. There was just one unscheduled pause caused by a cleric fainting.

Then, on impulse, Elizabeth moved towards the Tomb of the Unknown Warrior and gently laid down her bouquet of delicate roses. This was in memory of the brother who was not there on this her great day – Fergus, who had died at Loos. It had been planned that she should leave the bouquet at the Cenotaph on the way back to the Palace, and this gesture left her empty-handed for the long walk up the aisle.

At last the choir began to sing *Lead us heavenly father, lead us*, and Elizabeth and her father moved forward, with Elizabeth murmuring to him to keep his spirits up.

The ageing Archbishop of Canterbury, Dr Davidson, who had been Queen Victoria's Dean at Windsor, conducted the service. He invited the couple 'to make this one life now given to you something rich and true and beautiful'. The Archbishop of York, preaching the sermon, assured them that 'the warm and generous heart of this people takes you today into itself'.

As they walked from the Abbey to their fabulous Glass Coach with its imposing escort of cavalry, the sun broke through the clouds – an auspicious sign that this was destined to be the best of marriages. Elizabeth was now Her Royal Highness, the Duchess of York. As fourth lady in the land after the two Queens and her friend, Princess Mary, she was entitled to curtsies and all the other royal tributes.

A newspaper referring to the Duchess's informal style, waxed lyrical at the time saying: 'She drove to the Abbey in the simplest possible manner. On her return all was changed. From a commoner she became as if by magic, the fourth lady in the land . . .'

A Royal couple

The procession swept down Constitution Hill and into the Palace. There was something very appealing about the bridal couple: his clean-cut good looks complemented her wistful beauty and they looked so happy. The bride and bridegroom appeared on the balcony to acknowledge the cheers that swept towards them from the crowds. The wedding breakfast was held for 123 people, with 66 of the closest relatives seated at tables prettily decorated with Elizabeth's favourite pink tulips and white lilac, in the State Dining Room. The remaining guests dined in the Ball Supper Room.

The elaborate menu cards incorporating the crests of the Duke and Duchess told of many delicious courses: Consommé à la Windsor; Suprêmes de Saumon Reine Mary; Côtelettes

👑 *After the wedding, Elizabeth and Bertie left the Abbey in the State Glass Coach to go to Buckingham Palace* above. *Once inside, cheers from the crowd soon brought the couple out on to the balcony* right. *After the wedding breakfast, the newlyweds were showered with rose petals as they left for their honeymoon in an open landau* far right

Hulton-Deutsch Collection

👑 Elizabeth entered the Abbey at 11.30 am and, before walking up the aisle left, laid her bouquet on the Tomb of the Unknown Warrior. Then, after the wedding ceremony, and to the sound of Beloved, let us love one another, *they went to sign the register in the Chapel of Edward the Confessor. The register* inset is interesting for two reasons. The description of the King's occupation left hardly any room for Elizabeth's father to write his own, and – in her haste, or nervousness – the bride forgot to hyphenate her own name

Popperfoto

ILN Picture Library

♛ *Loyal subjects rushed to buy the special wedding edition of the* Illustrated London News, *which was produced to commemorate the royal wedding*

d'agneau Prince Albert; Chapons à la Strathmore; Jambon et Langue découpés à l'Aspic; Salade Royale; Aspèrges; Sauce Crême Mousseuse; Fraises, Duchesse Elizabeth; Pâtisserie; Fruits.

In the Green Drawing Room, the Duke and Duchess, using a silver knife, cut the enormous cake which had been made for them by McVitie & Price in Edinburgh.

Eventually, the couple left the Palace in an open landau drawn by four greys. All the guests were in high spirits and pelted them energetically with rose petals while the laughing Prince of Wales even managed playfully to hit Bertie square in the face with a screwed-up bag.

The honeymoon begins

At Waterloo Station, the couple climbed into a special carriage that had been attached to an ordinary train. In this glorious profusion of flowers, the couple sped away happily to the seclusion of Polesden Lacey in Surrey in the care of driver Wiggs.

In the grandeur of the Regency house deep in the country estate of society hostess the

Hon Mrs Ronnie Greville, Elizabeth and Bertie were at last alone at the end of a very long day. The happy couple spent ten days relaxing and playing golf – pleased to be on their own after the turmoil of the preparations and excitement of the day. And then they were off to Elizabeth's beloved Glamis on 7 May for the remainder of the honeymoon.

The honeymoon was not all roses, though. Poor Elizabeth succumbed to an attack of whooping cough – 'Not a very *romantic* disease', she complained.

The Countess had prepared a suite of three rooms for the honeymooners. When they arrived, Bertie's father, the King, wrote to him from Balmoral saying, 'The better I know and the more I see of your dear little wife the more charming I think she is and everyone fell in love with her here'. Elizabeth's gift of attracting and holding affection and love always enchanted everyone she met, but for Bertie it was more than enchantment – it was reality. It was here in the comfort, cosiness and security of a happy, caring home that Bertie at last understood the true meaning of complete contentment.

IN CELEBRATION

Before the start of their wedding reception, the Duke and Duchess of York happily posed for some wedding pictures. Elizabeth had chosen eight bridesmaids *below*, including her two nieces. They all wore ivory georgette dresses trimmed with Nottingham lace and leaf-green sashes, held at the waist by a white rose and a silver thistle. In their hair, they wore woven bandeaux of white heather and carried beautiful bouquets made up of

white roses and heather.

After their eight-course wedding breakfast, the Duke and Duchess cut their magnificent wedding cake *left*. It was 9ft high and weighed 800lb. There were four iced tiers. The lowest was decorated with their combined coats of arms, the second with the Strathmore arms, the third with the Duke of York's arms and the top tier displayed a vase of white flowers, symbolizing love and peace

Hulton-Deutsch Collection

Bassano/Camera Press

Popperfoto

'*She drove to the Abbey in the simplest manner. On her return all was changed. From a commoner she became, as if by magic, the fourth lady in the land. . . .*'

NEWSPAPER REVIEW

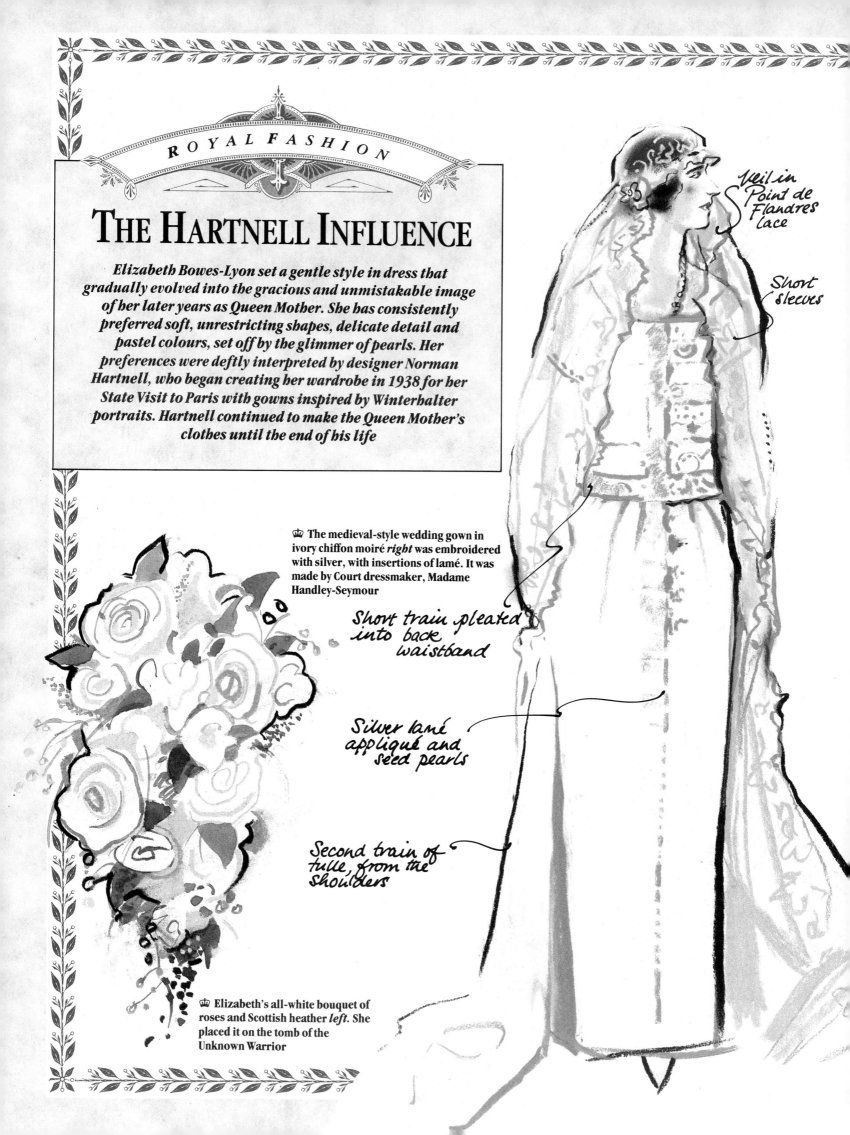

THE HARTNELL INFLUENCE

Elizabeth Bowes-Lyon set a gentle style in dress that gradually evolved into the gracious and unmistakable image of her later years as Queen Mother. She has consistently preferred soft, unrestricting shapes, delicate detail and pastel colours, set off by the glimmer of pearls. Her preferences were deftly interpreted by designer Norman Hartnell, who began creating her wardrobe in 1938 for her State Visit to Paris with gowns inspired by Winterhalter portraits. Hartnell continued to make the Queen Mother's clothes until the end of his life

♛ The medieval-style wedding gown in ivory chiffon moiré *right* was embroidered with silver, with insertions of lamé. It was made by Court dressmaker, Madame Handley-Seymour

♛ Elizabeth's all-white bouquet of roses and Scottish heather *left*. She placed it on the tomb of the Unknown Warrior

Veil in Point de Flandres lace

Short sleeves

Short train pleated into back waistband

Silver lamé appliqué and seed pearls

Second train of tulle, from the shoulders

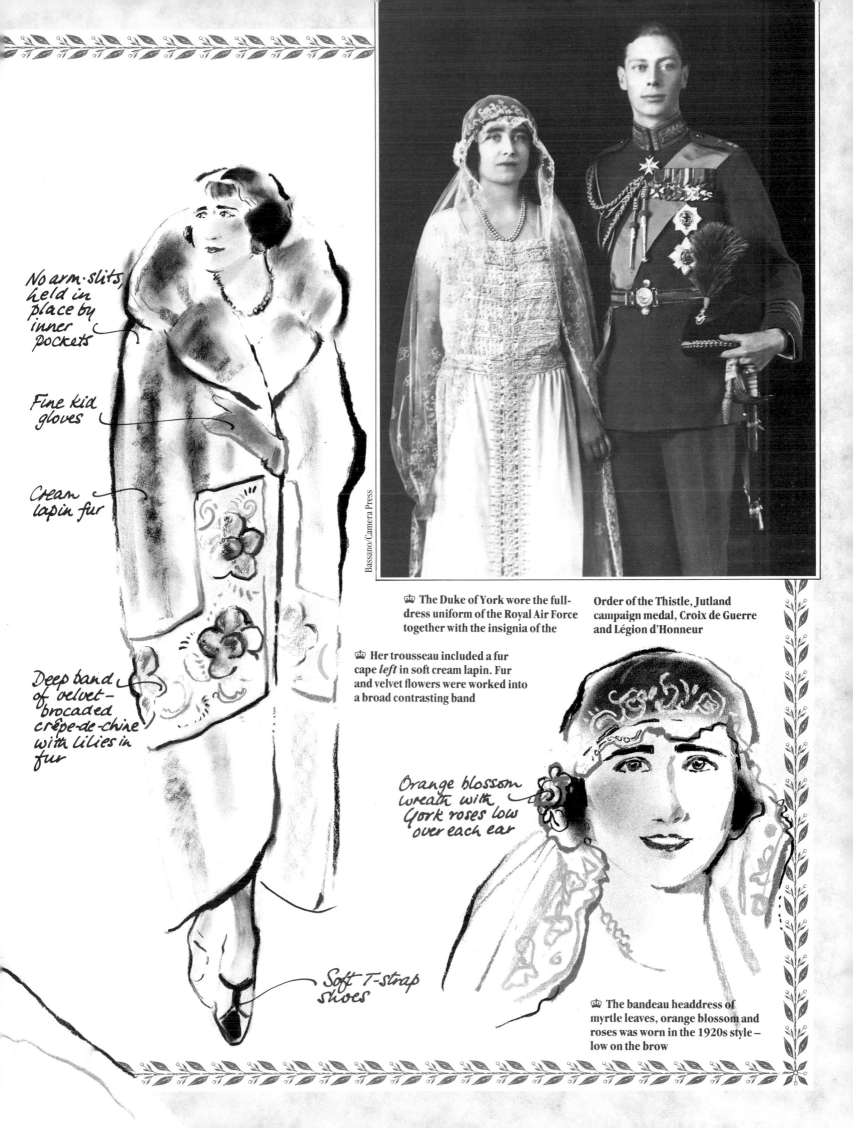

No arm-slits, held in place by inner pockets

Fine kid gloves

Cream lapin fur

Deep band of velvet-brocaded crêpe-de-chine with lilies in fur

Soft T-strap shoes

Bassano/Camera Press

♔ The Duke of York wore the full-dress uniform of the Royal Air Force together with the insignia of the Order of the Thistle, Jutland campaign medal, Croix de Guerre and Légion d'Honneur

♔ Her trousseau included a fur cape *left* in soft cream lapin. Fur and velvet flowers were worked into a broad contrasting band

Orange blossom wreath with York roses low over each ear

♔ The bandeau headdress of myrtle leaves, orange blossom and roses was worn in the 1920s style – low on the brow

♛ Elizabeth's country suit *left* in knitted silk, banded with silk braid, with link buttons. It is worn with a vivid coral blouse and suede hat

Cape-sleeved lace overblouse

Gently draped skirt

♛ Two off-the-face hats were deliberately selected by the Duchess who understood that her face always had to be visible to the public

♛ The softly-draped dress in black crêpe de chine and lace *right* was worn with a single string of pearls that were always Elizabeth's favourite accessory

Norman Hartnell

Specially designed for H.M. THE QUEEN

👑 Designs for day and evening *above* by Norman Hartnell were to set the Queen Mother's fashion style. He created her glamorous series of evening gowns, inspired by the work of portrait painter Franz Xaver Winterhalter. A typical design is the pretty white lace picture dress *below* with matching picture hat and frilly parasol

Cecil Beaton/Camera Press

Norman Hartnell

Single string of pearls

Asymmetrical one-button fastening

Corded quilting in scallop design

👑 The fur-trimmed 'dressmaker' suit *right* in light wool. The one-button jacket with fashionable asymmetric hemline is banded with scallops of corded quilting

'We always wanted a child to make our happiness complete'

GEORGE VI, ON THE BIRTH OF HIS
DAUGHTER ELIZABETH

Camera Press

Popperfoto

DUKE AND DUCHESS

THE ROYAL COUPLE'S HAPPINESS WAS MADE COMPLETE WITH THE ARRIVAL OF THEIR TWO DAUGHTERS. BUT THEIR CAREFREE FAMILY LIFE WAS SOON TO BE INTERRUPTED BY THE ABDICATION OF EDWARD VIII. THE SHY DUKE WAS SUDDENLY KING GEORGE VI

 In June 1923, White Lodge, in Richmond Park, became the first official residence of the Duke and Duchess of York. Although the 18th-century house was splendid in appearance, it had many disadvantages, including gas lighting, an inadequate water supply and draughty rooms that were impossible to heat. These difficulties – combined with the Yorks' increasing workload and the house's distance from London – were to make a move increasingly inevitable

W E MUST BREAK HER IN SLOWLY', observed King George V, anxious to allow Elizabeth an easy passage into royal life. But there was never to be the slightest hint of a problem. The new Duchess of York could always make people feel at ease, and even succeeded in bringing some joy and warmth into the lives of the rather staid King and Queen.

Dinners at Sandringham were very formal in the 1920s and the King, a stickler for punctuality, kept all the clocks half an hour fast to discourage latecomers. Early on, Elizabeth, never famous for her time-keeping, arrived two minutes late for a meal and the guests braced themselves for a royal explosion as Elizabeth apologized. 'You are not late, my dear', said His Majesty, 'I think we must have sat down two minutes too early.' Hushed astonishment greeted his words, but he qualified his attitude later, explaining, 'If she weren't late, she would be perfect, and how horrible that would be.'

To her husband who thrived on the security and serenity she brought into his life, she must have appeared perfect. Yet the relationship was not one-sided. Elizabeth, in turn, began to rely on Bertie's constant love and attention and a great partnership started to emerge.

The newlyweds set up their first home together at White Lodge, Richmond Park –

Country Life Books

A HOLIDAY TO REMEMBER

Their holiday in East Africa in 1924–5 was fondly remembered by Bertie and Elizabeth for the rest of their lives. Although, inevitably, there were a few official engagements, for four months the couple relaxed completely, adopting the casual dress of bush-shirts and floppy hats that was suitable for the tropical surroundings. These informal pictures, never published before, show them enjoying going on safari, game hunting, and the pleasures of outdoor life

Royal Commonwealth Society

Royal Commonwealth Society

Queen Mary's family home. But the house was some distance from London and attempts to rush back and change clothes between engagements could go disastrously wrong. The only thing that could be said in its favour was that the park's bracken and spotted deer reminded the couple of their beloved Scotland.

The Duchess undertook her first public appearance on 30 June 1923, when she accompanied the Duke to the Hendon Air Display to see the crack Squadron 39 whose planes boasted a top speed of 150 mph. Dressed in a fashionable pleated dress, her usual pearls and an eye-catching hat, her merry smile was a revelation to the 80,000 spectators who were more accustomed to the grave faces of the King and Queen – they thought it unseemly to appear light-hearted on public occasions. Elizabeth always took official duties in her stride and proved to be a huge success. Not surprisingly, her husband was overwhelmed with pride.

In 1924, a trip was planned for the Duke and Duchess to visit the Empire. Bertie was particularly keen to show Africa to Elizabeth. In December, they set off for several months and travelled on the SS *Mulbera* which carried the royal passengers to Mombasa on the East African coast. Both Bertie and Elizabeth adored the trip. Once royal duties and commitments were over, they spent four months on safari in both Kenya and Uganda enjoying some big game shoots.

The birth of a daughter

Shortly after their return to England, Elizabeth became pregnant, and she wanted to find a residence which was more congenial than White Lodge to welcome their first child. In a characteristically wise move, Elizabeth's mother, Lady Strathmore, offered them the family's London home in Bruton Street – an offer the couple accepted. This was the house from which Elizabeth had been married and it held many happy memories for her. On 21 April 1926, after a difficult labour, the Duchess gave birth to a girl – 'a little darling with a lovely complexion and pretty, fair hair, Queen Mary reported in her diary. She was christened Elizabeth Alexandra Mary, giving her the same initials as her mother, and the little Princess

♔ The births of Princess Elizabeth above *and Princess Margaret* below *were moments of supreme happiness for Elizabeth. But the demands of being wife to a prince of the realm meant that she was unable to devote herself to the children as much as she would have liked. Within weeks of Elizabeth being born, the Duchess was on a Royal tour lasting six months. The pain she felt leaving her daughters – on this or any subsequent tours – never eased*

became third in line of succession to the throne.

Bertie was besotted with his daughter and in his delight said, 'We always wanted a child to make our happiness complete.' But, as always, his first thoughts were for his precious wife. 'I am so proud of Elizabeth at this moment after all she has gone through during the last few days.'

King George V and Queen Mary hurried from Windsor to see their new grandchild, a liveried footman following them with a silver tray loaded with lilac and pink carnations. 'Lilibet', as she was known in the family, was a source of love and delight to her devoted grandparents, particularly the King.

Australia and New Zealand

Sadly, mother and daughter were soon to be parted. A royal tour had been arranged by the King for the Duke and Duchess who would act as his representatives at the opening of the Federal Parliament in the new capital of Australia, Canberra. The convention of those days decreed it unthinkable that the baby Princess would accompany her parents. Elizabeth was heartbroken, but resigned to her duty.

The tour was a triumph for Elizabeth. It was also a landmark for the Duke of York as he began to overcome his stammer. Elizabeth was determined that this problem should be resolved, and she persuaded the Duke to visit a speech therapist called Lionel Logue. Together she and Bertie struggled through many tongue-twisters and relaxing breathing exercises.

Bertie wrote to his mother from New Zealand: 'It all helped. I had to make three speeches this morning. The last one in the Town Hall was quite a long one, and I can tell you I was quite pleased with the way I made it, as I had perfect confidence in myself.'

The King was delighted with the success of the tour, and created Elizabeth a Dame Grand Cross of the OBE as a gesture of appreciation. Bertie had a new self-confidence and his father was full of admiration for his son's diligence.

Family contentment

The York family now had a town house of their own. Refurbished while they were away, 145 Piccadilly looked out over both Hyde Park and

Hulton-Deutsch Collection

Camera Press

👑 *With the heavy demands of public life, private family moments were rare, and as such were deeply treasured by both the Duke and Duchess*

Buckingham Palace Gardens from which King George would wave to 'Lilibet' spying on 'Grandpapa England' through her own personal set of binoculars.

On 21 August 1930, the Duke and Duchess had another daughter. Princess Margaret Rose made a late arrival at Glamis Castle — the first royal birth in Scotland since 1602. Little Princess Elizabeth, a chubby four year old, announced solemnly: 'I shall call her Bud ... you see, she isn't really a rose yet.'

The Duke of York, still an intensely private man, resolved that his growing family needed a weekend retreat. The King, when asked, agreed that the family might use Royal Lodge, which was a short distance across Windsor Great Park from the Castle.

Bertie was a genuinely keen and talented gardener, and the glorious confusion of rhododendrons, azaleas and rolling lawns that eventually formed the large garden of Royal Lodge was the creation of both the Duke and Duchess. All the family dogs would snuffle happily through the shrubbery. The Duchess's Tibetan Lion dog was named Choo Choo, because he made noises like a tiny train when he was a puppy, and the Princesses' corgi was called Dookie — his sharp teeth were the scourge of the household. He was chosen from three puppies because he had a tiny stump of a tail while the others (like most corgis) had no tails. 'Surely', said the Duchess, 'we must have the one which has something to wag. Otherwise, how can we know when he is pleased?' The Duke's yellow labrador was called Mimsy and she would rush to greet him every time she saw him. 'No house dogs in the palace' had

HOME ADDRESS

145 Piccadilly – the Yorks' family home for ten years – was a welcome relief after the discomforts of White Lodge. A comfortable four-storeyed house, it became a happy family home full of flowers, books, toys, as can be seen from the picture of the day nursery *below*. Its central location also brought Bertie and Elizabeth closer to their people. In the picture *right*, taken in 1927, they are shown with Princess Elizabeth, waving to crowds after their Australian tour

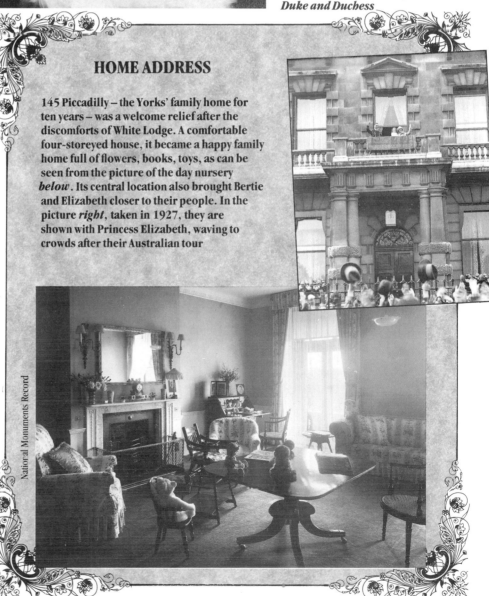

Syndication International

National Monuments Record

always been one of Queen Mary's strictest rules.

The Duke and Duchess adored their daughters who were supremely happy, and Bertie was determined that they should look back on their childhood as a golden time, in contrast to his own sad early years. With the help of the Royal Librarian, Elizabeth and Bertie wrote a personal history of the house they retrieved from neglect, including many maps, plans and photographs. The Royal Lodge was a real home, peaceful and not palatial, a home that they made themselves from the neglected and dilapidated old hunting lodge that they inherited from George IV's reign. No two people were ever happier than Bertie and Elizabeth as they created a warm and homely atmosphere of domestic bliss.

Celebrations then sadness

In the spring of 1935, the 70-year-old George V celebrated the Silver Jubilee of his reign as King. Many jubilee parties and celebrations went on throughout Britain and the Empire. Cheering crowds lined the streets on 6 May when King George and Queen Mary attended a thanksgiving service at St Paul's Cathedral.

Sadly, this was one of the King's last happy public events. Eight months later, he suffered a recurrence of bronchial trouble and died on 20 January 1936. The funeral took place at Windsor on 28 January.

♛ *The Duke and Duchess of York with the two young Princesses at King George V's*   *Silver Jubilee celebrations which took place in May 1935*

SPORTING ROYALS

Whenever possible, Bertie and Elizabeth found time to relax and indulge in their favourite interests. A natural sportsman from an early age, Bertie enjoyed a wide range of sports, including golf, polo, riding, hunting, and – a particular favourite – shooting. But it was at tennis that he really excelled, winning the RAF Doubles competition with his partner Louis Greig in 1920. (Both went on to enter the championships in 1926, but were beaten in three sets.) Elizabeth always went to watch Bertie on such occasions, to provide her usual moral support, but tended to favour more leisurely pursuits. Here, she snatches a moment on tour in New Zealand to indulge in one of her favourite pastimes – fishing

THE RELUCTANT MONARCH

With the death of his father, the popular Prince of Wales was proclaimed King and, using one of his other names, became Edward VIII. A rather tense relationship had existed between the Prince and his father. George V felt that royalty should retain an aura of mystery among the people. The young prince, however, did not agree and, with his modern education, felt that attitudes should be changed.

Sometimes indiscreet and flippant, he chose older, married women for companions and confidantes. Although well-loved by the people, he also began to reflect on the nature of his public role: 'Lonely drives through tumultuous crowds, the almost daily inspection of serried ranks of veterans, the inexhaustible supply of cornerstones to be laid ... sad visits to hospital wards, every step bringing me face to face with some inconsolable tragedy . . . always more hands to shake than a dozen princes could have coped with.'

Troubles ahead

Saddened though Bertie was by the death of his father, he was revelling in family life and cherishing his role as father to his two young daughters. As the couple divided their time between 145 Piccadilly and Royal Lodge, Windsor, they were blissfully unaware of the looming events that were going to change their lives for ever.

King Edward VIII had only reigned for a few months when severe constitutional problems began to surface. For several years now, he had been friendly with the divorced American, 40-year-old Wallis Simpson, and the relationship continued to develop to such an extent that he announced his intention to marry her. Despite continued pressure to do his royal duty and give up the woman he loved, the King remained immovable about his intention to marry, and renounced his right to the throne. On 10 December 1936, The Instrument of Abdication was drawn up, and Edward VIII became the first King to abdicate in Britain since Richard II in 1399. In the early hours of 12 December, he left England on HMS *Fury* tortured by many conflicting loyalties and emotions. He went to live in exile in France and eventually married his dear beloved Wallis on 3 June 1937.

On the day of the abdication, Saturday 12 December, Bertie became King George VI,

THE ABDICATION CRISIS

As George V lay in state in Westminster Abbey, a constitutional crisis began that would make history. Edward VIII's friendship with twice-divorced American Wallis Simpson - previously a minor irritation – now assumed prime importance as he announced his decision to marry her. On 11 December, Edward announced his decision to relinquish the throne. He sailed to France the next morning to join Wallis, and they were married the following June. In later years, he recalled, 'Watching the shores of England recede, I was swept by many emotions. If it had been hard to give up the Throne, it had been even harder to give up my country'

John Frost

Popperfoto

Popperfoto

Topham Picture Library

choosing his fourth Christian name as he intended to rule in the same style as his father. His first speech as King was spoken in a quiet, nervous voice and it ended with him saying, 'With my wife and helpmate by my side, I take up the heavy burden which lies before me.' His obvious distress was highlighted in a later comment, 'I'm only a naval officer, it's the only thing I know about.'

The new King opted for the same date already arranged for his brother's coronation, saying sardonically, 'Same date, different King.'

The coronation

Ten-year-old Princess Elizabeth found the events all rather puzzling. She had seen a letter addressed to 'Her Majesty the Queen'. 'That's Mummy now, isn't it?' she asked a footman tentatively. Her young sister, Margaret Rose, was simply cross. 'I had only just learnt to spell Y-O-R-K,' she piped angrily. Their father was aghast when they first curtsied to him, and perhaps it was only at that moment he fully realized that nothing could ever be the same again. 'I never wanted this to happen, I'm quite unprepared for it,' he protested to his cousin Louis Mountbatten. His wife was far more determined, however, and confided to the Archbishop of Canterbury, 'The curious thing is we are not afraid.'

Coronation Day, 12 May 1937, was a tremendous ordeal for Bertie, and he looked ghost-white as he emerged from the State Coach at Westminster Abbey. Soon, he was joined by Elizabeth, who walked bareheaded into the church with dignity and pathos, wearing a dress that shimmered with the symbols of the Empire embroidered on heavy white satin in diamanté. To many of the guests at this thousand-year-old sacred ritual, the moment before Bertie was anointed and robed for the crowning was most touching of all, as he knelt at the altar rails, quite alone – a symbol, perhaps, of the loneliness of the monarchy. Yet after his coronation, there seemed to be a distinct change in him – he suddenly acquired the regal pose of a King. Those who watched may have begun by pitying him and worrying for him, but before long, they came to respect him totally.

Time to celebrate

After the ceremony, the new King and Queen, wearing their crowns, rode through the crowded London streets to Buckingham Palace. The pouring rain did nothing to dampen anyone's spirits. The King and Queen made five appearances on the balcony, waving to the throng of people below. Then, in slow measured tones, the King broadcast a speech to his people on the radio saying 'The Queen and I will always keep in our hearts the inspiration of this day.'

His final act in this long and taxing day was to demonstrate his loving thanks to Elizabeth by giving her the Thistle Badge and Star, making her the only Lady of the Thistle ever. He had designed the emblem himself, and this perfect gift of finest diamonds, sapphires and emeralds symbolizing their love affected Elizabeth so much that she lost her voice.

The new sovereigns

After the pomp and splendour of the coronation, the King and Queen were thrown into a ceaseless round of work.

Elizabeth did all she could to lighten the King's burden, and life in their new home at Buckingham Palace retained an extraordinary degree of continuity with that of 145 Piccadilly. There were still family weekends at The Royal Lodge with the peace of gardening, family games like racing demon, charades and rummy and quiet times listening to the radio. One of their guests expressed his admiration for the new Queen: 'I cannot tell you how superb she was. What astonished me is how the King has changed. He is now like his brother. He was so gay and she so calm...'

One of their first trips abroad – a State Visit to France – was planned. It was the first since 1914, but disaster struck as the King and Queen were about to depart. Lady Strathmore, the Queen's dearly-loved mother, suffered a fatal heart attack and, with Bertie and Elizabeth at her bedside, she died.

Elizabeth was grief-stricken and everyone, including the President of France, assumed that the visit would be postponed. Elizabeth would not cancel the trip, however, and was determined to do her duty. Norman Hartnell, the royal dressmaker, pointed out to the King that white was a colour of mourning and designed a wardrobe of thirty white, nostalgic dresses inspired by Winterhalter portraits. The King was delighted with the outfits and from the moment Elizabeth opened her delicate white parasol, republican France fell captive to her charms. Headlines proclaimed, 'We have taken the Queen to our hearts. She rules over two nations, France is a monarchy again!'

THE CORONATION OF GEORGE VI

ILN Picture Library

John Frost

Camera Press

Crowds lined the route to catch a glimpse of George VI and Queen Elizabeth on the way to their Coronation at Westminster Abbey on 12 May 1937. After the shock of the abdication, the British people took their new sovereigns to their hearts. Parties were held all over the country and countless commemorative articles were produced in celebration

Stanley Gibbons

Phillips Auctioneers

ROYAL LODGE, WINDSOR

One and a half miles across the Great Park from Windsor Castle lies a beautiful pink-walled house. Originally built as a hunting lodge for George IV, Royal Lodge was badly neglected until, in 1931, George V presented it to the Duke and Duchess of York as a grace and favour country home. The couple lovingly restored the house to create a haven of peace and tranquillity where they could retreat with their family from the cares and strains of their royal duties. Bertie was to derive particular pleasure from the huge grounds, which developed his interest as a keen amateur gardener

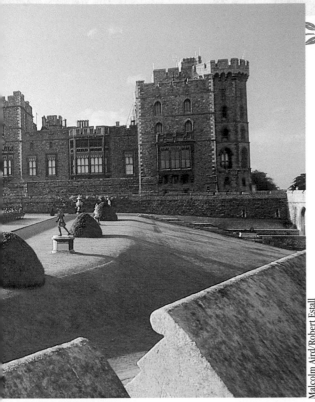

Malcolm Aird/Robert Estall

Country Life Books/Paul Hamlyn Publishing

♛ Furnished in the informal style of a typical English country house, the Octagon Room *below* is ideal for relaxation. The Queen Mother's writing desk *left*, crowded with her personal treasures, stands near the French windows where she can enjoy the view of the garden that she and Bertie created together

Country Life Books/Paul Hamlyn Publishing

Country Life Books/Paul Hamlyn Publishing

Hulton-Deutsch Collection

♛ The first recorded house built on the site of Royal Lodge was Lower Lodge, for many years the home of Thomas Sandby who was Ranger of the Great Park. The garden provided a wonderful relaxation area for Bertie and Elizabeth, both together and with their growing family *left*

All: Country Life Books/Paul Hamlyn Publishing

👑 The Wyatville Saloon *above* and *left* is the main room that survives from the reign of George IV. It is 48 feet long, 29 feet wide and 20 feet high. Five great windows lead on to the terrace with its views of spreading lawns and woodlands. Over the fireplace hangs a portrait of George IV by Sir Thomas Lawrence

👑 Situated just behind the Lodge is The Little House (Y Bwthyn Bach) *opposite top*. This perfect miniature of a traditional Welsh cottage was presented to Princess Elizabeth on her sixth birthday in the name of the children of Wales. The building is two storeys high and only 15 feet tall. It is completely furnished to scale, and even includes a bathroom with running water

♛ Very close to the Royal Lodge, the Royal Chapel *right* was built by George IV and it is here that the Royal Family worships when they are in Windsor. (St George's Chapel is only used on special occasions.) The family use a box pew in the chancel which screens them from the rest of the congregation, but the chancel arch pillar was cut back to enable George VI to have a better view himself

♛ *The bombing of Buckingham Palace gave Bertie and Elizabeth a personal taste of the horrors of war. But they were unstinting in their efforts to keep up the spirits of their people whether it was women working in a Berkshire field, London's blitzed Eastenders or children in a London rest centre*

Camera Press

Sport and General

BBC Hulton Picture Library

CHIL... DIN...

IN WAR AND PEACE

IN THE DARK DAYS WHEN THE NATION'S VERY EXISTENCE WAS THREATENED, BERTIE AND ELIZABETH BECAME SYMBOLS OF THE BRITISH SPIRIT. BUT AS VICTORY DAWNED, THE KING WAS ALREADY LOSING HIS PERSONAL BATTLE AGAINST ILL-HEALTH

O N CHRISTMAS DAY, 1939, KING GEORGE VI spoke to the nation: 'I said to the man who stood at the Gate of the Year, "Give me a light that I may tread safely into the unknown".'

The message echoed everyone's feelings about the increasingly tense and terrifying mood in Europe, and his comforting broadcasts on the BBC radio brought a new intimacy between the King and his people. Such occasions, of course, filled Bertie with dread because these were the days of live broadcasting, but Elizabeth joined him as he settled in front of the microphone, and went through the script with him. One BBC engineer, a Mr Woods, was a great help on these occasions and became something of a legend. When the Queen was trying to change the script, so that the words would be easier for Bertie to say, Mr Woods would agree wholeheartedly, saying, 'You're preaching to the perverted, Ma'am.'

'He's coming along magnificently,' Ramsay Macdonald told the Queen as they both listened to George VI speaking at a public function. 'And how am I doing?' she asked. 'Oh, you ...' said the former Prime Minister, leaving her in no doubt of his complete approval. Politicians from all parties acclaimed the accomplished way in which the King and his Queen Consort had moved to centre-stage in world affairs.

After the deceptive hopes of Neville Chamberlain's visit to see Hitler in Munich, it still seemed safe for the King and Queen to embark on a long-planned visit to the United States and Canada in May 1939. It was the first visit by a reigning British monarch and the aim was to enlist support in the event of war. They travelled across Canada in six weeks from coast to coast, and then there was a four-day stay in America where President Roosevelt was their host in Washington.

The visit was a triumph which was to have far-reaching effects for Britain in the darkest days of World War 2.

To a distinguished Guildhall audience, Bertie delivered an emotional speech describing the trip, which was interpreted in Europe as a declaration of Britain's intention to defend her institutions to the end, if need be. 'It was interesting,' wrote an observer, 'to watch the effect of his words on such hardened experts as Winston Churchill, Baldwin and the Archbishop of Canterbury. It was patent that each of them, and indeed everybody in that historic place, was deeply moved.' The King's old friend, Louis Grieg, wrote to congratulate him, to which Bertie replied, 'It was a change from the old days when speaking, I felt, was "hell".'

Finally, and inevitably, the shaky peace dissolved. The King's voice spoke over the radio with that sombre, measured emphasis that added poignancy to all his public words. 'For the second time in the life of most of us,' he said, 'we are at war.'

Shelter from the stormy blast

Elizabeth and Bertie were a centre of calm for the whole nation at a desperately needed moment of crisis. London was pounded by enemy bombs and the mournful wailing of the air raid

> ## *'I'm glad we've been bombed; now we can look the East End in the face'*
> QUEEN ELIZABETH, AFTER THE AIR RAID ON BUCKINGHAM PALACE

♛ *The war years, despite the suffering they caused, did much to enhance the reputation of the Royal Family. With his stammer and slightly nervous air, Bertie did not at first seem ideally suited to the role of wartime leader. But his courage and morale-boosting efforts, aided by the support of Elizabeth, soon won the monarchy the nation's respect and admiration. So much so that at the end of the war, Winston Churchill was to be moved to write: 'This war has drawn the Throne and the people more closely together than ever recorded, and Your Majesties are more beloved by all classes and conditions than any of the princes of the past'*

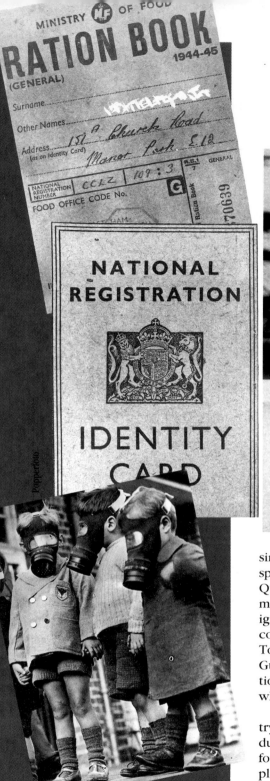

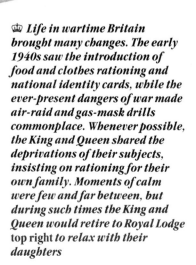

👑 *Life in wartime Britain brought many changes. The early 1940s saw the introduction of food and clothes rationing and national identity cards, while the ever-present dangers of war made air-raid and gas-mask drills commonplace. Whenever possible, the King and Queen shared the deprivations of their subjects, insisting on rationing for their own family. Moments of calm were few and far between, but during such times the King and Queen would retire to Royal Lodge top right to relax with their daughters*

siren seemed endless. At the moment when spirits were at their lowest, the King and Queen would appear, suddenly and quite informally, picking their way through the rubble, ignoring the dust and the stench to bring encouragement and to give hope to everybody. Together they visited ARP Centres, Home Guard stations, barracks, hospitals and munitions centres – they even shared bomb shelters when they were caught in an air raid.

The King inspected the damage to Coventry Cathedral the morning after the Blitz had reduced it to a shell. He and the Queen had a profound respect for the heroism of ordinary people in these bitter years.

'There was a marvellous spirit, you know,' said the Queen remembering. 'One used to feel so sad at the destruction and loss of life – on the other hand, everyone was in such marvellous form that one came home feeling rather comforted. It must have been very hard at times, especially in the East End.' However, she said with a triumphant smile, 'the Cockney's a good fighter, and he fought back!' In their turn, the people admired the King and adored his wife.

Buckingham Palace remained the centre of royal authority throughout the war, although the King and Queen spent most nights and some weekends at Windsor Castle where the Princesses had been taken for their safety. 'Who is this Hitler spoiling everything?' the furious nine-year-old Margaret Rose demanded to know. It had been suggested that the royal

family should leave the country, but Elizabeth scotched that idea quickly. 'The children could not go without me, I could not possibly leave the King and the King would never go.'

Surviving the Blitz

Finally, their Majesties shared with their compatriots the experience of being bombed. The Queen remembers Friday, 13 September 1940 vividly. 'We were in this little room looking out over the quadrangle where the King worked quite a lot during the war.' Here, she pauses for a characteristic aside that highlights her intense compassion for Bertie, and her complete understanding of his sensitivity. 'Actually, the sun came into it which made a difference, you know . . . We heard this 'plane coming down the Mall. There wasn't any warning at all, and then this extraordinary scream that a bomb makes. The first one exploded in the quadrangle not very far from us. He dropped a great stick right across the Palace and the only one that did very much damage was a direct hit on the chapel which caught it rather badly.'

To hit the Palace was the aim of every Luftwaffe pilot but, strangely enough, when the royal couple inspected the damage, the Queen said 'I'm glad we've been bombed; now we can look the East End in the face.' But there were lighter moments too. When an explosion hit the drainage system, the garden was flooded with rats and everyone had great fun chasing and shooting them. By the end of the war, she

KEEPING UP MORALE

The King and Queen's wartime morale-boosting efforts were unequalled as they travelled thousands of miles – at home and abroad – to offer encouragement to the troops. Much of the time, they were separated. The Queen is shown *right* visiting the wounded from Dunkirk in an English hospital and the King is photographed *far right* looking at the Maginot line with a French officer as early as December 1939

Hulton-Deutsch Collection

Topham Picture Library

recalled, 'there were no windows left at all. Poor old house!'

The King and Queen journeyed half a million miles about the country, often in great personal danger despite the precautions of bullet-proof cars and the King's sten gun concealed in a despatch case. 'I think they liked my coming to see them in their adversity', he told his diary with characteristic diffidence after visiting the survivors in Coventry. Sometimes, the tours kept them away for two weeks at a time. 'I feel quite exhausted after seeing and hearing so much sorrow,' the Queen told Queen Mary, but she and her husband never broke down – they kept their self-control, although it tired them even more.

The King and Queen also suffered personal tragedies during the war but, like everyone else, they had to absorb the pain and carry on with their duties. Prince George, the Duke of Kent and Bertie's youngest brother, was killed in an air crash and the Princess Royal's son was

Popperfoto

captured by the Germans. In 1944, Lord Strath-more died at the age of 89 at Glamis. He had been devoted to his youngest daughter, and she to him. It was a hard blow for the Queen.

Towards the end of the war, between June 1943 and October 1944, King George VI went abroad to visit the battle fronts. He visited North Africa, France, Italy, Malta and the Low Countries. 'He feels so much at not being more in the firing line,' the Queen had written in a letter to Queen Mary.

Finally, when the King and Queen were utterly exhausted by the rigours of everything they had gone through, the long years of the war drew to a close. On 8 May 1945, Winston Churchill joined them on the balcony of Buckingham Palace to celebrate victory in Europe with the hundreds of thousands of cheering people below who yelled in exhilaration, 'We want the King! We want the Queen!' At times during the war, the royal couple had seemed one person, so close had they become.

♛ *On VE day, 8 May 1945, the crowds thronged outside Buckingham Palace calling for the King and Queen and their family. In the centre of the group was Winston Churchill who gazed serenely at the thousands celebrating below the balcony. The war was over*

Popperfoto

Popperfoto

🐾 *The photograph top of George VI and Queen Elizabeth with Princess Elizabeth and Princess Margaret during their tour of South Africa in January 1947 is a historic one. This was the only time the monarchs were accompanied by their daughters on an overseas visit. It also provided the Princesses with a foretaste of the duties that were to become an important feature of their official lives. The royal family returned to England in April. A few months later, in July, months of speculation were ended with the announcement of Princess Elizabeth's engagement to Philip Mountbatten – a moment of particular personal joy for Bertie and Elizabeth after the troubled war years*

AFTER THE VICTORY

O n 15 August 1945, the King broadcast to his people: 'The war is over. Our hearts are overflowing, as are your own. Yet there is not one of us who has experienced this terrible war who does not realize that we shall feel its inevitable consequences long after we have all forgotten our rejoicings.' His Majesty's BBC broadcasts had been a rallying point for his people during the war, but all the effort and stress had taken a terrible toll on his less than robust health.

'I feel burned out,' was his frequent comment and the daunting problems of post-war reconstruction meant that the 'intolerable burden' of his kingship was scarcely lightened. He resorted to wearing tan make-up for public appearances to disguise the tell-tale signs of exhaustion. He described his dilemma to his brother Henry, the Duke of Gloucester. 'I am perfectly well really, but feel that I cannot cope competently with all the varied and many questions which come up.' He began to rely more and more on his Queen.

In 1947, a royal tour of South Africa was planned, involving the whole family. It was soon noticed by all how tired the King was. Soon, the high temperatures were bothering him and he started to suffer cramps in his legs and began to lose weight. Elizabeth always soothed him, encouraged him and saved him as his irritation boiled over – 'gnashes' the family called his outbursts of temper.

Happy family life

Before leaving England, Princess Elizabeth had implored her parents to allow her to become engaged to the dashing young lieutenant, Philip Mountbatten. Although the family had known the exiled Prince from Greece for the last seven years, the King and Queen had in-

sisted that she wait until her twenty-first birthday. They wanted her to be absolutely sure of her choice because they knew from their own experience that when the Princess was Queen she would have only one really close confidant, and that would be her husband. The Princess celebrated her twenty-first birthday with a ball in Cape Town and a month after the family's return to England, still sure of her love for Philip, the engagement was announced. Later the same year Elizabeth and Philip were married.

In the spring of 1948, Elizabeth and Bertie celebrated 25 years of married life with a Silver Wedding Thanksgiving Service in St Paul's Cathedral. In the evening, they each broadcast to the nation. 'Looking back over the last 25 years and to my own happy childhood,' said the Queen, 'I realize more and more the wonderful sense of security and happiness which comes from a loved home.'

The King's ill health

As spring turned to summer, the pains in the King's legs had given him a great deal of trouble, and by autumn he was forced to take to his bed to forestall the danger of gangrene and amputation caused by arteriosclerosis. At first, he was so tired that he was content to rest. He managed to work his way through the Red Boxes in bed, determined that Princess Elizabeth should not be worried as she awaited the birth of her first child in another wing of the Palace. The Queen divided her time between her two charges, and on 14 November, the Princess gave birth to a son, the royal monarchs' first grandchild, Prince Charles.

For a while, it seemed as if Bertie's health would improve, and becoming a grandfather seemed to have had a relaxing effect. But when he was told that his right leg was still obstructed and that he needed surgery, the old temper flared. 'So all our treatment has been a waste of time,' he roared. He adamantly refused to go to hospital: 'I have never heard of a King going to hospital.' The operation was performed in March 1949 to relieve the obstruction, and was successful.

The Queen and Princess Elizabeth took over his engagements, but someone as committed to duty as George VI found it almost impossible to sit on the sidelines. He insisted on attending the Trooping of the Colour, but the Queen persuaded him to sit in an open carriage watching Princess Elizabeth take the salute from her horse.

In the summer of 1950, the Queen sent Bertie to Balmoral again when Princess Elizabeth was due to have her second child. She realized that the tension and waiting would be

Baron/Camera Press

♛ *By the late 1940s, the King's health was giving serious cause for concern, and he was barely well enough to pose for the official photograph* right *taken to celebrate his Silver Wedding in 1948. The picture* below – *taken three years later, with Elizabeth, Prince Charles and Princess Anne – shows a visible deterioration. This was the first time the King had been photographed since his operation to remove a lung. He was to die a few months later*

too much, and he would be on the telephone every other minute to Clarence House where the Princess lived. The baby was late, proving the Queen right, and Princess Anne arrived on 14 August 1950.

The King had no choice but to heed his physicians' advice and ease up on his demanding state duties to avoid the risk of thrombosis. Although he was well enough to attend the opening ceremonies of the Festival of Britain in May 1951, lung X-rays showed a 'shadow' and it was diagnosed that he had lung cancer. In October that year, his left lung was removed, for a malignant growth had been found. The King was never to know the seriousness of his condition.

Elizabeth was torn between her public duties and her private cares. Shattered by Bertie's illness, she took on more and more of the Sovereign's work as a Counsellor of State, continuing with her own programme and comforting Bertie on his particularly bad days.

The last goodbye

At the very end of January 1952, the King and Queen went to Heathrow airport to say goodbye to Princess Elizabeth and Prince Philip who were visiting Australia on their behalf, stopping in Kenya on the way. Bareheaded in the biting wind, the King stood on the tarmac looking frail and sad as the aeroplane disappeared into the distance. Elizabeth tried to distract him with talk of their immediate plans – a visit to Sandringham. The King called himself a Norfolk man and liked nothing better than to shoot. 'You've had your fun. Now I am going to have mine,' he told his doctors, and with a special light gun with a heavier charge, he pitted his skill against the game at the Keeper's Day shoot on 5 February.

Later, he discussed the day with Elizabeth and Princess Margaret who had been to lunch with local artist, Edward Seago. Then Margaret

👑 *George VI waved a last goodbye to Princess Elizabeth and Prince Philip at Heathrow airport, after seeing them off when they left for their tour of Australia and New Zealand. This was the last time Princess Elizabeth saw her father alive*

👑 *As the body of George VI lay in state in Westminster Hall, the nation mourned a much-loved King. For three days and in freezing temperatures, crowds of people queued to pay their last respects. The queue – six deep – stretched along the north bank of the Thames, over Lambeth Bridge, along the Embankment to St Thomas's Hospital. Over 300,000 mourners passed through Westminster Hall*

the parents' royal tour. Comforted by their innocent chattering, she explained, 'I have got to start sometime, and it is better now than later.'

Naturally, her control gave way in private. One friend, commenting on how Elizabeth disguised her sorrow, was told, 'Not when I am alone.' 'Sorrow', she wrote to another, 'bangs one about until one is senseless.'

On the evening before the King was to be buried at Windsor, Elizabeth went alone to Westminster Hall where he was lying in state. She arrived just before midnight and stood in the shadows, never taking her eyes off the purple-draped catafalque.

On the day of the funeral, Friday, 15 February 1952, the coffin was covered with the Royal Standard and all the royal regalia – the Imperial

played the piano and they listened to a news report on the royal trip to Kenya. The King went twice to the kennels to inspect his gundog's injured paw and then to bed at 10.30, saying, 'I'll see you in the morning.'

In the early hours of 6 February, he suffered a fatal coronary thrombosis.

Elizabeth became a widow and 'felt engulfed by great black clouds of unhappiness and misery.' The axis of her life was gone. During their marriage, she and Bertie had almost never been parted, but now she was alone. The moment an equerry told her that the King had died in his sleep she said, 'I must go to him.' A vigil was to be kept at the door of his bedroom: 'The King must not be left,' she ordered.

Buffeted by grief

Her Majesty astonished her household with her courage. 'I never knew a woman could be so brave', said one of them in admiration. Although almost broken by grief, she went as usual that evening to play with her grandchildren, Prince Charles and Princess Anne, who had been left in their grandparents' care during

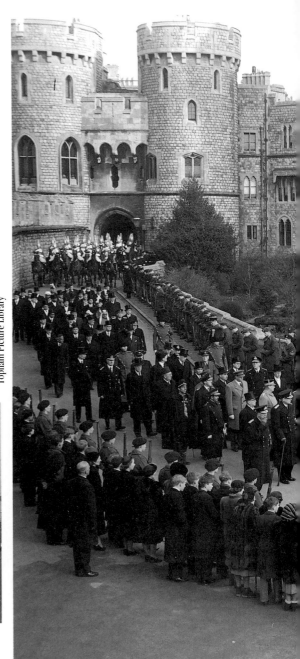

State Crown which had weighed so heavy on Bertie during the coronation, the orb and sceptre, the insignia of the Order of the Garter and Elizabeth's white flowers bearing the tribute, for 'my dear husband, a great and noble King.'

The gun carriage bearing the coffin was drawn through the cold winter's morning past 145 Piccadilly where, as Duke and Duchess of York, Elizabeth and Bertie had spent the happiest of times with their children before they had to take on the heavy responsibilities of monarchy.

As the coffin was lowered into the vault in St George's Chapel with Elizabeth's flowers still in place, the new Queen had to be supported by her mother. The heavy mantle of the monarchy now rested on her young shoulders. No-

one knew better than Bertie's Queen what a burden that could be. Her husband had never been strong, and he paid the highest price for dedicating himself heart and soul to the role history called on him to play.

Three days after the funeral, King George's consort and widow, still comparatively young at the age of 51, issued a personal statement in which she declared, 'Throughout our married life we have tried, the King and I, to fulfil with all our hearts and with all our strength the great task of service that was laid upon us. My only wish now is that I may be allowed to continue the work we sought to do together.'

The King was laid to rest at St George's Chapel, Windsor below left. Although Elizabeth showed great self-control and royal composure at his funeral, her sorrow at his death never left her. She is shown below mourning with Queen Mary and her daughter Elizabeth, the new Queen

PORTRAIT OF A MARRIAGE

Queen Elizabeth, the Queen Mother, has a host of mementoes and treasures with which to look back over her life, among which are her pictures and jewellery, her china collection and the beautiful Castle of Mey on the north coast of Scotland. Each item provides a record of joy, love and sadness, both of her love affair with her beloved Bertie and her own life which has spanned nearly a century

Pilgrim Press

♛ A fine collection of Meissen porcelain at Glamis Castle *left* inspired a lifetime's interest in this beautiful style. Two more Meissen vases can be seen in the painting *right*

ILN Picture Library

♛ The lovely miniature *above* was treasured by Bertie all his life. It was a wedding gift from Elizabeth's mother, the Countess of Strathmore, and was painted by Mrs Mabel Hankey. The family portrait *right* called 'Conversation Piece' is a perfect picture of domestic peace. It was painted by Sir James Gunn in 1950, just two years before the death of the King. The Queen Mother always has this room at Royal Lodge repainted in the same shade

By Courtesy of The National Portrait Gallery London

Tim Graham

👑 It was during the sad weeks following her husband's death that the widowed Queen discovered the Castle of Mey *above*, then called Barrogill Castle. It was a 16th-century Scottish ruin, but years of loving care have since restored it to its former rustic glory

👑 The Queen Mother has a large collection of lapel brooches and is particularly fond of this pearl and diamond flower with its delicate loop of diamonds and teardrop pearl *right*. It was originally given to Queen Victoria by her Household

Tim Graham

Photographers International

BELOVED GRANDMOTHER

AFTER THE IRREPARABLE LOSS OF HER DEAR HUSBAND, ELIZABETH BEGAN TO BUILD HERSELF A FULFILLING NEW LIFE. SHE CREATED A ROLE THAT HAD NEVER EXISTED BEFORE, AND ENDEARED HERSELF TO ALL AS THE QUEEN MOTHER

Snowden/Camera Press

Photographers International

O N 2 JUNE 1953, THE QUEEN MOTHER DROVE in a glass coach with Princess Margaret to Westminster Abbey for the Coronation of her elder daughter, Elizabeth. She was to become only the second Queen in British history (Queen Mary was the first) to watch the crown being placed on the head of her child. Glittering from top to toe in diamonds, she regally played the second lead. Perfectly composed as ever, she walked slowly up the aisle to William Walton's *Orb and Sceptre* played on the organ, bowing to familiar faces in the congregation. She took her place in the front row of the Royal Gallery along with her four-year-old grandson, Prince Charles, whom she kept fortified with barley sugar as she unravelled some of the intricacies of the service to him.

The new Queen soon found that her mother's constant advice and good humour was just the strength and support she needed in her new, difficult task and has said, 'She has been the most marvellous mother, always standing back and never interfering.' Once, when lunching with her mother in the library of Clarence House, the Queen thought she might just allow herself a glass of wine. 'Is that wise?' her mother enquired teasingly, 'You know you have to reign all afternoon.'

At the birthday thanksgiving service for the Queen Mother's 80th birthday held in 1980 at St Paul's Cathedral, it was the Queen's wish to stay in the background as much as possible — not an easy thing to do when one is Head of State. On this day, she accorded her mother two very special privileges. The first was for the Queen Mother to have the Sovereign's escort of the Household cavalry to and from St Paul's, and the second was for her to be the last to arrive there, and the first to leave. Tutored by King George V in the true art of royal protocol,

♛ *Greetings from young admirers on her 83rd birthday* above. *Clarence House* right *is the Queen Mother's 'town house' and it is from here that she conducts her official duties. She moved in from Buckingham Palace in 1952, only a few weeks before her daughter's coronation*

Tim Graham

the Queen Mother was all too aware of this honour.

Although quite different personalities, their respect for each other is total. An immense capacity for hard work is one characteristic they share. They also share a profound love of outdoor life and the British countryside.

Fishing for salmon has been the Queen Mother's life-long hobby and pleasure in Scotland and abroad. During long summer holidays in the highlands of Scotland, many picnics are held, however cold it is, and it has not been unknown for the Queen Mother to sing one of her favourite old songs with a warming drink in her hand, waiting for Prince Philip to cook something delicious on the barbecue.

At home with the next generation

She is very fond of all her grandchildren and great-grandchildren, and she has always been there to give supportive love and advice. She gave much-needed solace to the young Prince Charles — her favourite — in his troubled school days at Gordonstoun. Viscount Linley and Lady Sarah also sought her comfort and protection when Princess Margaret's marriage to Lord Snowdon was breaking up.

Her irrepressible sense of fun and her sharp wit have been passed on to the Prince of Wales, perhaps tempering his mother's sense of dedication and his father's irascibility.

The Queen Mother has never been known to be spartan in her tastes. Birkhall, her country

Photographers International

♛ *The Queen Mother best understands the new roles that her granddaughters-in-law* above *have had to assume. Holding Prince Henry* left, *a great-grandchild*

Norman Parkinson/Camera Press

home near Balmoral, is a beacon for the younger members of the Royal Family, and for years she has given a party for them and their friends in September, in this large, white Queen Anne house. Lady Diana Spencer sought refuge there from snooping lenses before she and the Prince of Wales were married, and Prince Andrew and Sarah Ferguson relished the same privacy before they were engaged.

Although the Queen Mother loves country pursuits, she is a sophisticated lady and is just as much at home in the elegance of the city as she is in Scotland or at the racecourse.

Following her move from Buckingham Palace in 1952, she established herself in Clarence House and, with her dedicated staff of 40, quickly transformed it into one of the most stylish houses in London. It was from here that Princess Margaret married Antony Armstrong-Jones in 1960. And later, Clarence House and the Queen Mother were to provide hospitality for her two granddaughters-in-law, Lady Diana Spencer in 1981 and Sarah Ferguson in 1986.

In the house, she has a fine display of silver, including the dessert service made for Queen Charlotte in 1787. She also has a fine art collection containing pictures by Monet, Lowry, Sickert, John Piper and Duncan Grant. A whole room is given over to the works of the Norfolk artist, Edward Seago.

Regular visitors at Clarence House prize above all things the delicious food and the excellent champagne that is served.

Dealing with the media

Over recent years, as royalty have been featured more in the Press, the Queen Mother has proved a natural when dealing with the photographers and reporters who follow her every public move. She is the most professional of all the royals as far as they are concerned, and they add that she is quite delightful – high praise indeed from such determined individuals. Norman Parkinson, Her Majesty's favourite photographer, fondly recalls the time when he photographed the Queen Mother in the Drawing Room of Clarence House for her 75th birthday portraits. She wore a formal gown of white

♛ *In 1980, Elizabeth's 80th birthday was celebrated with much public and private rejoicing* right. *The sparkle and joy of this happy occasion have been caught by favourite photographer, Norman Parkinson. For this famous, but unorthodox portrait* far right, *the royal mother and daughters wore their capes back to front*

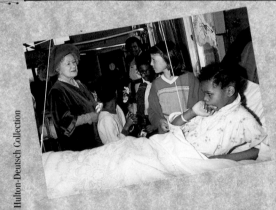

Hulton-Deutsch Collection

'WE COULDN'T SPARE MUMMY'

Not long after Queen Elizabeth II came to the throne, it was suggested to her that the Queen Mother might be the perfect candidate for the Governor-Generalship of Australia or Canada. 'Oh I'm afraid not,' was the Queen's emphatic and speedy reply. 'We couldn't possibly spare Mummy.' Looking at the workload she has handled shows just how right this decision was. The Queen Mother is patron of some 300 organizations and charities, Colonel-in-Chief of eight British regiments,

Commandant-in-Chief of all three Women's Services and Lord Warden of the Cinque Ports.

A genuine, caring curiosity about people is, she finds, the prime requisite. But whenever possible, she tries to derive the most enjoyment from it. When she was in Venice in 1984, she found her gondola ride, '*Magnifico! Magnifico!*'

'Work', she believes, 'is the rent we pay for our place on earth.' As a result, no one begrudges her passion for racehorses

Hulton-Deutsch Collection

Norman Parkinson/Camera Press

Allsport Photographic Ltd

Tim Graham

chiffon embroidered with gold beads – the sort of dress that has become her trademark – with her favourite necklace, a wedding present from Edward VII to Alexandra, and the 'new' tiara, made in 1953 by Cartier from diamonds presented to Edward VII in 1901. 'Mr Parkinson,' she said, 'why don't I behave like one of your models?' and twirled about as the photographer caught the essence of her personality. 'Parks' was delighted: 'The Queen Mother is quite exceptional. She has now returned to a state of bloom – a quick radiance.'

Her Majesty was once asked if she were aware that her empathy is almost tangible. She confessed, 'I must admit, I do, at times, feel something flowing out of me. It makes me very tired for a moment; then, I get something back from the people, sympathy, goodwill – I don't know exactly – and I feel strength again, in fact recharged.'

Exciting trips

One of the Queen Mother's overseas visits ('my little jaunts') was to Venice in 1984, at the invitation of the 'Venice in Peril' Fund. It was, for her, the fulfilment of a long-held ambition to revisit that glorious city. She was thrilled to have a ride in a gondola. 'It would have been a shame to have come here without being able to take a spin,' she said.

Another slightly surprising method of travel for a great-grandmother was her private supersonic 85th birthday present from British Airways. Having heard that the Queen Mother

was very keen to fly on Concorde, they whisked her away for a 100-mile trip over England, Scotland and the North Sea. She spent much of the flight tucked into the tiny cockpit talking to the crew and marvelling at the wonders of modern science. She also thoroughly approved of her in-flight meal of lobster and champagne.

She is National Hunt racing's most respected owner. 'Ma'am is an expert,' confirms her Private Secretary and long-time racing companion, Martin Gilliatt. Indeed, as one sports journalist shrewdly observed, 'If there's a shorter cut to a bloody nose in Tattersall's than to criticize the Queen Mother in any way, I do not know it.' Her 86th year saw this enthusiast enjoying an excellent season and in April 1986, she threw a party at Clarence House to celebrate three magnificent wins in one day at Sandown. She invited her trainers, Fulke Walwyn and Ian Balding, together with their wives, and also the three stable lads responsible for looking after each of the victors, along with other racing friends. For probably the hundredth time, they all settled down happily to watch videos of the horses, Special Cargo, Insular and The Argonaut, gallop past the winning post.

A castle of one's own

It was soon after Bertie's death that, far away from London, the Queen Mother discovered 16th-century Barrogill Castle, now called the Castle of Mey. A tiny castle, the most northerly

Snowdon/Camera Press

♛ Ranger steals the show – almost – and lends a characteristic touch of informality to Elizabeth's official portrait by Lord Snowdon, taken for her 87th birthday

in Britain, it is situated on the cliffs facing Scapa Flow where Bertie served as a naval officer. She spotted the derelict building from a road above it, quite by chance. 'I thought, Oh dear, I must try and save it – so I took it on!' She built it up gradually over 12 years into her own personal summer home.

Life at the Castle of Mey

The Queen Mother likes to gaze out to sea from her bench on the shore, and when the winds force her inside, she watches her favourite video, *Rumpole of the Bailey*. Often, she climbs into the Land Rover well rugged up against the gales to set off for Thurso to chat to the owner of the local antique shop, and then stops to take a walk with Ranger, her beloved corgi. Then, she returns home to enjoy a relaxing evening.

For the best part of her life, the Queen Mother has been in excellent health. In her later years, she inevitably suffers some ailments, such as the ulcerated leg that troubled her a great deal in the early 1980s.

Although she has a great interest in homeopathy and prefers these natural remedies to taking any prescribed drugs, in the mid-1960s she underwent major surgery for the first time when she had a colostomy operation. She recovered rapidly, determined to get well enough to resume her normal life.

On her own

Queen Elizabeth, the Queen Mother, is the most loyal of friends and as she gets older, her greatest sadness is that she has outlived so many of her dearest companions, particularly her brother, David, and the late Sir John Betjeman, the Poet Laureate, who had been a great friend. They shared the same sense of humour, and used to go on excursions to the tiny country churches they both loved so well.

From childhood, Elizabeth understood that any kind of relationship, however fleeting or however meaningful, requires application and hard work from both sides. A clever woman with a true genius for her job, Her Majesty's deep self-awareness and her self-indulgence help to give her a clear perception of how to deal with the rarified world of the monarchy in conjunction with the more down-to-earth ways of the democratic world outside. As a friend says, 'People who know how to please themselves know how to please others.'

A time to remember

Elizabeth has been a widow longer than she was a wife, but she has created exactly the life that Bertie would have wanted for her out of her early loneliness and desolation. By applying herself to her duties, her family and friends, she veiled her loneliness and gave of herself unstintingly. However, certain dates are always left unfilled in her diary – her husband's birthday, the anniversaries of their marriage and his death. These are days that she keeps for herself – days when she is alone to remember and treasure the happiness they shared.

History has never turned simply on great events of social or political evolution: personalities are equally important, and it has been said that the personality of the Queen Mother is the main reason why Great Britain still has a monarchy when so many other countries have abandoned their royal houses and traditions. George VI was forced to take Edward VIII's place as King, but the character of Elizabeth his wife, with her unique style, considerable intelligence and powerful instincts, has shaped the future of the House of Windsor.